JR. GRAPHIC MONSTER STORIES

THE LOCH NESS MONSTER!

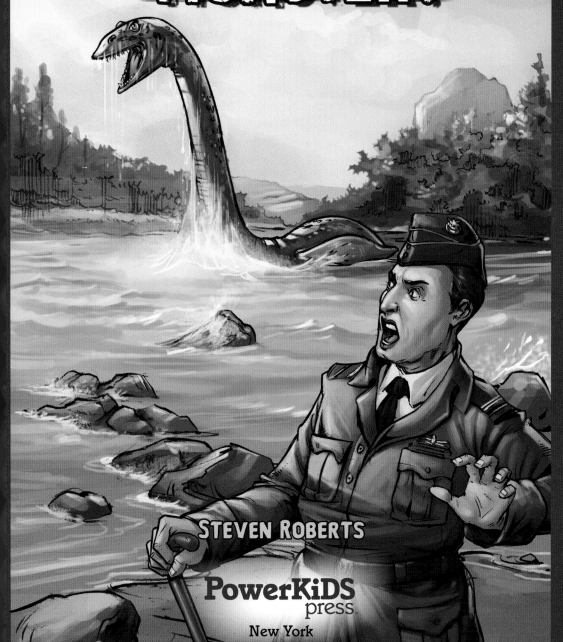

STEVEN ROBERTS

PowerKiDS
press

New York

Published in 2013 by The Rosen Publishing Group, Inc.
29 East 21st Street, New York, NY 10010

First Edition

Editor: Joanne Randolph
Book Design: Planman Technologies
Illustrations: Planman Technologies

Library of Congress Cataloging-in-Publication Data

Roberts, Steven, 1955-

The Loch Ness monster! / by Steven Roberts. — 1st ed.

　　p. cm. — (Jr. graphic monster stories)

Includes index.

ISBN 978-1-4488-7904-5 (library binding) — ISBN 978-1-4488-8004-1 (pbk.) — ISBN 978-1-4488-8010-2 (6-pack)

1. Loch Ness monster--Juvenile literature. I. Title.

QL89.2.L6R63 2013

001.944—dc23

2012005776

Manufactured in the United States of America

CPSIA Compliance Information: Batch # SW12PK: For Further Information contact Rosen Publishing, New York, New York at 1-800-237-9932

Contents

Main Characters   3

Loch Ness Monster Facts   3

Loch Ness Monster!   4

More Scottish Monsters   22

Glossary   23

Index and Websites   24

Main Characters

Alex Campbell (1930s) In 1933, he wrote and published an account of the sighting of the **Loch Ness monster**.

Tim Dinsdale (1924–1987) Beginning in the 1960s, he led over 50 expeditions to find the Loch Ness monster.

C. B. Farrel (c. 1940s) Claimed to have seen the Loch Ness monster in 1943 while on duty in the service of the British military.

Robert Rines (1922–2009) In the 1970s, used advanced **technology** in an effort to locate and photograph the Loch Ness monster.

Loch Ness Monster Facts

- The Loch Ness monster has been nicknamed Nessie. It is said to be 40 to 50 feet (12–15 m) long. It is described as having a long neck like that of a huge lizard, a head like a horse's, and up to two humps on its back.
- Loch Ness, where the Loch Ness monster is said to live, is a huge lake. It is about 23 miles (37 km) long and 1 mile (2 km) wide. Loch Ness is up to 786 feet (240 m) deep at its deepest point. It lies about 50 feet (15 m) above sea level. Loch Ness is connected to the sea through the River Ness.

Loch Ness Monster!

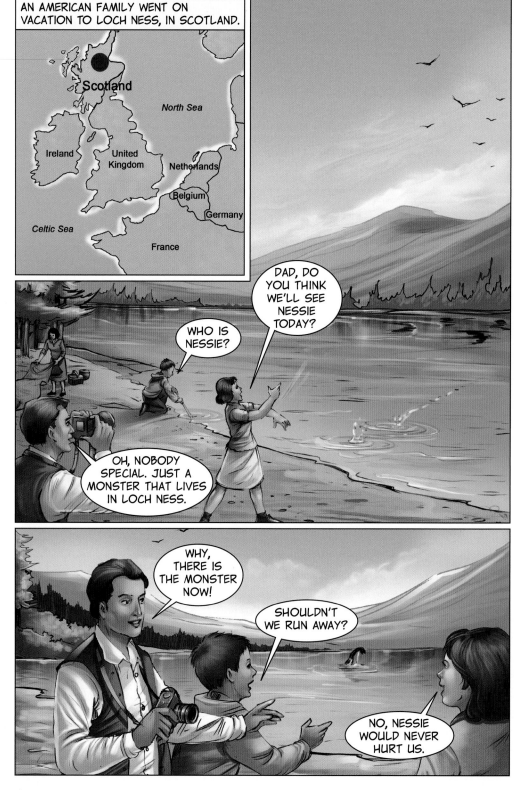

"THE FIRST MODERN SIGHTING OF NESSIE WAS IN 1933, WHEN TWO INNKEEPERS, MR. AND MRS. MACKAY, SAW SOMETHING IN THE **LOCH**."

WHAT DO YOU THINK THAT IS?

IT LOOKS LIKE SOME DUCKS ARE FIGHTING.

MAYBE IT'S A GIANT FISH.

OR A WHALE.

"THE INNKEEPERS TOLD ALEX CAMPBELL WHAT THEY HAD SEEN. HE WAS IN CHARGE OF FISHING IN THE LOCH."

IT WAS RIGHT THERE, ROLLING AROUND AND SPLASHING.

IT WAS ENORMOUS.

I'LL HAVE TO INVESTIGATE.

THIS IS AMAZING!

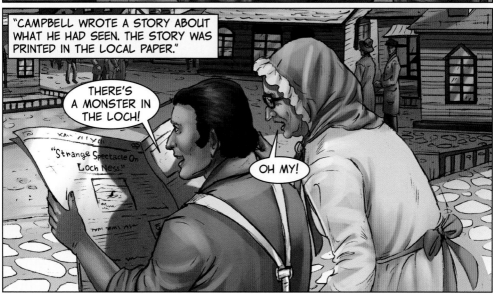

"CAMPBELL WROTE A STORY ABOUT WHAT HE HAD SEEN. THE STORY WAS PRINTED IN THE LOCAL PAPER."

THERE'S A MONSTER IN THE LOCH!

"Strange Spectacle On Loch Ness!"

OH MY!

"THAT SAME YEAR, GEORGE SPICER AND HIS WIFE SPOTTED THE MONSTER ON LAND."

GEORGE, STOP THE CAR!

WHAT IS THAT THING?

I'M TELLING EVERYONE ABOUT THIS.

I HOPE THEY BELIEVE US.

IN APRIL 1934, DR. ROBERT KENNETH WILSON TOOK A PICTURE OF THE MONSTER.

PULL OVER, ROBERT. THERE'S SOMETHING IN THE WATER.

IT'S A MONSTER!

LET ME GET THIS ON FILM.

"DR. WILSON'S PHOTOGRAPH BECAME FAMOUS ALL OVER THE WORLD. IT BECAME KNOWN AS THE 'SURGEON'S PHOTOGRAPH.'"

"SEVERAL YEARS LATER, THE ROYAL AIR FORCE EXAMINED DINSDALE'S FILM."

IT COULD BE A FISHING BOAT.

BUT LOOK HOW IT WENT UNDER THE WATER. BOATS DON'T DO THAT.

"THE ROYAL AIR FORCE CAME OUT WITH ITS REPORT. IT SAID THE FILM SHOWED SOMETHING THAT WAS PROBABLY ALIVE IN THE LOCH."

WE HAVE THE PROOF WE NEED TO KEEP LOOKING.

WELL DONE!

"OVER THE YEARS, DINSDALE LED MORE THAN 50 EXPEDITIONS TO FIND THE LOCH NESS MONSTER. HE SPOTTED IT TWO MORE TIMES BUT DID NOT HAVE A CAMERA WITH HIM EITHER TIME.

"IN THE 1960S, THE LOCH NESS INVESTIGATION BUREAU WAS FORMED. IT HAD MORE THAN 1,000 MEMBERS WHO **MONITORED** THE LAKE AROUND THE CLOCK.

"THEY ALSO USED **SONAR** AND **SUBMARINES** TO LOCATE THE MONSTER.

"THE SEARCHERS WERE DISAPPOINTED. MOST OF THEIR PHOTOS TURNED OUT TO BE WATER BIRDS."

JUST A BIRD AGAIN!

"IN 1987, THE LARGEST UNDERWATER SEARCH OF THE LOCH TOOK PLACE. IT WAS CALLED OPERATION DEEP SCAN."

AS YOU CAN SEE BEHIND ME, THESE BOATS WILL BE SWEEPING THE LOCH TODAY. THEY'RE USING A SPECIAL KIND OF SONAR.

I FOUND AN OBJECT.

SO DID I!

ME TOO!

"AFTER DAY ONE, EVERYONE WAS EXCITED. HOWEVER, DAY TWO WAS DISAPPOINTING. NONE OF THE OBJECTS COULD BE FOUND AGAIN."

I THOUGHT WE'D SEE THE MONSTER.

YEAH, I DON'T THINK IT EXISTS.

"WHAT COULD THE MONSTER BE? THERE ARE MANY DIFFERENT THEORIES. SOME THINK IT'S A TYPE OF **DINOSAUR** CALLED A **PLESIOSAUR.**

"OTHERS BELIEVE IT'S AN ORDINARY FISH OR ANIMAL, LIKE A LARGE RIVER **OTTER.**

More Scottish Monsters

- **The Supernatural Water Kelpie**
Many tales have been told of the water **kelpies**, or water horses, which haunt the lochs and rivers of Scotland. Their skin is deep green, and they have black tails and manes. You can tell a water horse by its constantly dripping mane. A kelpie will stand on the shore, saddled and bridled, luring small children to climb on its back for a ride. As soon as they mount what they thought was a horse, though, they stick to its skin. The kelpie then plunges into the icy depths of the loch, where the children drown and are then eaten.

- **Taming the Kelpie**
With their strength, speed, and ability to take other shapes, kelpies almost always get the better of their victims. Sometimes, though, they can be defeated and tamed. The ability to change forms is contained within a special bridle. The owner of this bridle controls the kelpie and can bend it to his will. The Clan MacGregor, an ancient Scottish family, is said to possess such a bridle, passed down from one generation to the next after an ancestor tamed a kelpie near Loch Slochd.

- **A Saintly Sighting**
One of the earliest tales of Scottish monsters involves St. Columba, who came to western Scotland from Ireland to convert the native Picts to Christianity in AD 563 .The story goes that Columba ventured out one day and came across a group of men burying a friend. They told Columba that the man had been swimming in the river when a great monster swam up, grabbed him, and bit him. He then died of his wounds. Columba asked his assistant to swim across the river. Awakened by the splashing, the monster reared up out of the water and began to attack. Columba stood tall, raised his hands, and said, "Thou shall go no further, nor touch the man; go back with all speed." The monster shrank back and swam away as quickly as it had come.

Glossary

dinosaur (DY-nuh-sawr) Any of a group of extinct reptiles that includes the largest-known land animal.

documentary (do-kyuh-MEN-tuh-ree) A movie or a television program about real people and events.

enhanced (in-HANTSD) Made better or easier to see.

hoax (HOHKS) Something that has been faked.

investigate (in-VES-tuh-gayt) To try to learn the facts about something.

kelpies (KEL-peez) Legendary Scottish water spirits or water horses.

loch (LOK) The Scottish word for a large lake.

Loch Ness (LOK NES) A lake in the Highlands of Scotland near the town of Inverness.

Loch Ness monster (LOK NES MON-ster) A large, dinosaur-like creature that, according to legend, lives in Loch Ness, in northern Scotland.

monitored (MO-nuh-turd) Observed and recorded something.

otter (O-ter) A small mammal that lives in water.

plesiosaur (PLEE-see-uh-sawr) An ancient extinct reptile that lived in water.

sonar (SOH-nahr) A way of using underwater sound waves to find objects or judge distances.

submarines (SUB-muh-reenz) Ships that are made to travel underwater.

technology (tek-NAH-luh-jee) The way that people do something using tools and the tools that they use.

Index

D

Dinsdale, Tim, 3, 12, 13, 17

documentary, 17, 23

E

expedition, 3, 10, 13

F

Farrel, C. B., 3, 11

flipper, 15, 17

H

hoax, 19, 23

I

innkeeper, 6, 7

L

lizard, 3

Loch Ness, 3, 4, 13, 14, 19, 20, 23

M

monster, 3, 4, 5, 7, 8, 9, 10, 11, 12, 13, 14, 16, 17, 18, 19, 20, 22, 23

R

River Ness, 3

S

Scotland, 4, 22, 23

sonar, 14, 15, 16, 17, 23

Spicer, George, 8

submarines, 14, 23

Websites

Due to the changing nature of Internet links, PowerKids Press has developed an online list of websites related to the subject of this book. This site is updated regularly. Please use this link to access the list:

www.powerkidslinks.com/mons/loch/